MW01047082

HERmiletics The Workbook
Homiletics for Women in Ministry

DR. CYNTHIA MCINNIS

HERmiletics The Workbook: Homiletics for Women in Ministry

Copyright ©2024 by Cynthia McInnis

All rights reserved. This book or any portion thereof may not be reproduced or used in any manner without the publisher's express written permission except for brief quotations in critical reviews and specific noncommercial uses permitted by copyright law.

Printed in the United States of America First Printing, 2024
ISBN: 978-1-7338592-8-8

BALM2 Productions, Inc.
Brooklyn, NY

Special thanks to Wanza Leftwich of Leftwich Press for her invaluable assistance in publishing this book.

DEDICATION

To the women who taught me everything I need to know about
what I need to know. There is no me without these.

Mom Beverly McInnis,
taught me how to successfully merge marriage and
ministry, raising a family, and being a lady while I'm at it.

Pastor Josephine Batts (a.k.a Aunt Phine),
introduced me to the God of the BIBLE and how to rightly divide His word.

My mom, Mary Johnson,
my best supporter and daily reminder that I matter to God, and I matter to
His people. You kept me from quitting when things got rough.

CONTENTS

What is Homiletics?

Homiletics is the art and science of preparing and delivering sermons or religious speeches. It stems from the Greek word "homilia," which means conversation. In essence, homiletics focuses on the effective communication of spiritual truths and teachings to a congregation or audience.

Homiletics involves studying various aspects such as biblical interpretation, sermon structure, rhetorical techniques, and public speaking skills. It is not just about delivering a message but also ensuring that the message is engaging, relevant, and impactful to the listeners. By mastering the art of homiletics, preachers and religious leaders can effectively convey their message and inspire positive change in the lives of their audience.

Overall, homiletics plays a vital role in the field of religious studies and helps individuals communicate their beliefs and teachings in a compelling and persuasive manner. By understanding the principles of homiletics, individuals can enhance their preaching skills and connect with their audience on a deeper level.

Key Lesson Concepts:

- Homiletics is the art and science of preparing and delivering sermons or religious speeches.
- It involves studying biblical interpretation, sermon structure, rhetorical techniques, and public speaking skills.
- Homiletics helps individuals effectively communicate spiritual truths and teachings to a congregation or audience.

The Importance of Homiletics in Preaching

Homiletics is the art and science of preaching. It plays a crucial role in delivering effective and impactful sermons that resonate with the audience. By studying homiletics, preachers can learn how to effectively communicate the message of the Gospel, engage their listeners, and inspire spiritual growth.

Homiletics helps preachers develop their preaching skills, such as crafting compelling messages, delivering with clarity and conviction, and connecting with the congregation on a deeper level. Through the study of homiletics, preachers can enhance their ability to deliver sermons that inspire, challenge, and encourage their listeners in their spiritual journey.

Overall, understanding the importance of homiletics in preaching is essential for preachers who want to make a meaningful impact on their congregation. By honing their preaching skills through the study of homiletics, preachers can effectively communicate the transformative power of the Gospel and inspire positive change in the lives of their listeners.

Key Lesson Concepts:
- Homiletics is the art and science of preaching

- Preachers can learn how to effectively communicate the message of the Gospel through the study of homiletics
- Homiletics helps preachers develop their preaching skills and connect with their congregation on a deeper level

Section Summary

Homiletics is the art and science of preparing and delivering sermons or religious speeches, rooted in the Greek word "homilia," meaning conversation. It involves:

- Studying biblical interpretation
- Understanding sermon structure
- Learning rhetorical techniques
- Developing public speaking skills

Homiletics aims to effectively communicate spiritual truths and teachings to an audience, focusing on engagement, relevance, and impact. By mastering homiletics, preachers can inspire positive change and connect deeply with listeners.

Key Lesson Concepts of Homiletics include:

- Homiletics is the art and science of preparing and delivering sermons
- It is crucial for effective and impactful sermon delivery
- Preachers can learn to communicate the Gospel effectively through homiletics
- Homiletics helps preachers develop key preaching skills and connect with their congregation

NOTES

NOTES

Women in Preaching Throughout History

In this lesson, we will explore the significant role women have played in the history of preaching. Despite facing numerous challenges and obstacles, women have been influential preachers throughout the ages, using their voices to inspire and empower others.

We will examine key figures such as Sojourner Truth, who fought for both women's rights and the abolition of slavery through her powerful speeches, as well as modern-day trailblazers like Joyce Meyer and Beth Moore, who have impacted millions through their preaching and teaching ministries.

By studying the contributions of women in preaching throughout history, we gain a deeper understanding of the importance of diverse voices in spreading the message of faith and hope. This lesson will challenge us to appreciate the unique perspectives and insights that women bring to the pulpit and inspire us to continue breaking down barriers in the field of preaching.

Key Lesson Concepts:

- Women have played a significant role in the history of preaching.
- Key figures such as Sojourner Truth, Joyce Meyer, and Beth Moore have made a lasting impact through their preaching.
- Studying the contributions of women in preaching inspires us to value diverse voices and break down barriers in the field.

Challenges Faced by Female Preachers in History

Throughout history, female preachers have faced numerous challenges in their quest to spread their messages and serve their communities. From societal expectations to religious restrictions, these women have overcome significant barriers to practice their faith and fulfill their callings.

One of the main challenges female preachers have faced is the patriarchal structure of many religious institutions. Women have often been marginalized and excluded from leadership roles within churches, mosques, and temples. This has made it difficult for women to gain credibility and support as spiritual leaders.

Additionally, female preachers have had to navigate social norms and cultural biases that question their authority and capabilities. Many have had to fight against stereotypes and discrimination in order to be taken seriously in their roles as religious teachers and guides.

Key Lesson Concepts:

- Patriarchal structure of religious institutions
- Marginalization and exclusion from leadership roles
- Social norms and cultural biases

Section Summary

In this lesson, we will delve into the significant role that women have played in the history of preaching, despite facing various challenges and obstacles. Women throughout the ages have been influential preachers, using their voices to inspire and empower others.

- We will examine key figures such as Sojourner Truth, who fought for women's rights and the abolition of slavery through her powerful speeches.
- We will also explore modern-day trailblazers like Joyce Meyer and Beth Moore, who have impacted millions through their preaching and teaching ministries.

Studying the contributions of women in preaching helps us appreciate the importance of diverse voices in spreading messages of faith and hope. It challenges us to value unique perspectives and insights that women bring to the pulpit and motivates us to break down barriers in the field of preaching.

Throughout history, female preachers have encountered numerous challenges in their efforts to spread their messages and serve their communities.

- One of the main challenges has been the patriarchal structure of many religious institutions, where women have been marginalized and excluded from leadership roles.
- Female preachers have had to navigate social norms and cultural biases that questioned their authority and capabilities, leading to stereotypes and discrimination.

This has made it difficult for women to gain credibility and support as spiritual leaders, emphasizing the need to address the issues of patriarchal structures, marginalization, and biases within religious contexts.

NOTES

NOTES

Feminist Hermeneutics and Homiletics

In this lesson, we will explore the intersection of feminist theory with hermeneutics and homiletics. Feminist hermeneutics is an approach to interpreting religious texts that emphasizes women's perspectives and lived experiences. It challenges traditional patriarchal interpretations and seeks to uncover hidden voices and stories of women in the text. Homiletics, on the other hand, is the art of preaching and communicating the message of the text to a congregation. By combining feminist hermeneutics with homiletics, we can create more inclusive and empowering sermons that resonate with all members of the church community.

Throughout this lesson, we will discuss the importance of feminist perspectives in interpreting religious texts and how it can enrich our understanding of scripture. We will also explore different methods and tools that can be used to incorporate feminist hermeneutics into the preaching process. By the end of this lesson, you will have a deeper appreciation for the role of feminist hermeneutics in shaping the way we interpret and communicate the message of the text in a church setting.

Key Lesson Concepts:
- Understanding feminist hermeneutics and its significance in interpreting religious texts
- Exploring the intersection of feminist hermeneutics with homiletics in the preaching process
- Incorporating feminist perspectives into sermon preparation and delivery for a more inclusive and empowering message

Deconstructing Gender Bias in Preaching

In this lesson, we will explore the pervasive issue of gender bias in the realm of preaching. We will examine how traditional gender roles and stereotypes have influenced the way in which individuals perceive and evaluate sermons delivered by men and women. By deconstructing these biases, we aim to promote a more inclusive and equitable preaching environment.

We will discuss the impact of gender bias on the evaluation of preaching style, content, and delivery. Through critical analysis, we will challenge the misconceptions and prejudices that often accompany gender bias in preaching. By raising awareness and promoting dialogue, we hope to foster a more diverse and accepting space for all individuals to share their spiritual messages.

By the end of this lesson, students will have a deeper understanding of the ways in which gender bias manifests in preaching and how it can be dismantled. Through reflection and discussion, participants will be equipped with the tools and knowledge to combat bias in their own preaching practices and create a more inclusive environment for all voices to be heard.

Key Lesson Concepts:
- Examine the impact of traditional gender roles on perceptions of preaching
- Challenge misconceptions and prejudices related to gender bias in preaching
- Empower participants to create a more inclusive preaching environment

Section Summary

In this lesson, we will delve into the intersection of feminist theory with hermeneutics and homiletics in interpreting religious texts:
- Feminist hermeneutics emphasizes women's perspectives, challenges patriarchal interpretations, and uncovers hidden voices of women in texts.
- Homiletics focuses on preaching and communicating the text's message to a congregation.
- Combining feminist hermeneutics with homiletics can lead to more empowering and inclusive sermons.

- We will discuss the importance of feminist perspectives in scripture interpretation and explore methods to integrate feminist hermeneutics into preaching.

Key Lesson Concepts:
- Understanding feminist hermeneutics and its significance in interpreting religious texts.
- Exploring the integration of feminist hermeneutics with homiletics in the preaching process.
- Incorporating feminist perspectives into sermon preparation and delivery for a more inclusive message.

This lesson also addresses the issue of gender bias in preaching:
- Examination of how traditional gender roles influence perceptions and evaluations of sermons by men and women.
- Deconstructing biases to create a more equitable preaching environment.
- Discussion on the impact of gender bias on preaching evaluation regarding style, content, and delivery.
- Challenging misconceptions and prejudices associated with gender bias in preaching through critical analysis.

Key Lesson Concepts:
- Examining the influence of traditional gender roles on preaching perceptions.

- Challenging misconceptions and prejudices related to gender bias in preaching.
- Empowering participants to foster a more inclusive preaching environment through awareness and dialogue.

NOTES

NOTES

Choosing a Topic and Text

When diving into the world of hermeneutics, one of the first steps is selecting a topic and text to focus on. The topic sets the theme and direction for your study, while the text provides the material for analysis and interpretation. Carefully choosing a topic and text can shape the entire course of your study and research.

Consider selecting a topic that resonates with your interests and passions, as this will keep you motivated and engaged throughout the process. Additionally, choose a text that is rich in content and open to various interpretations. Be open-minded and willing to explore different perspectives and meanings within the text, as this will enhance your understanding and critical thinking skills.

Remember that the topic and text you choose should be challenging yet manageable. Strive to find a balance between complexity and accessibility, allowing yourself room to explore and expand your knowledge while also staying grounded in the fundamental concepts of hermeneutics.

Key Lesson Concepts:

- Choose a topic and text that resonate with your interests and passions
- Select a text that is rich in content and open to various interpretations
- Strive for a balance between complexity and accessibility in your choice of topic and text

Structuring a Sermon for Impact

Creating a sermon that deeply impacts your audience requires careful planning and structure. In this lesson, we will explore the key elements of structuring a sermon for maximum impact. By following these guidelines, you will be able to deliver a message that resonates with your listeners long after the sermon is over.

The first step in structuring a sermon for impact is to clearly define your main message or theme. This central idea will serve as the foundation for your entire sermon and will guide the rest of your planning process. Next, you will need to outline the main points that support your message. These points should be clear, concise, and relevant to your audience. Finally, consider how you will engage your listeners throughout the sermon. Using stories, examples, and interactive elements can help keep your audience engaged and connected to the message.

Key Lesson Concepts:

- Define a clear main message or theme

- Outline supporting main points
- Engage listeners with stories, examples, and interactive elements

Section Summary

Developing a unique and effective preaching style is crucial for aspiring preachers. It is not only about the words you use but also about how you deliver them and the impact they create on your audience. Here are the key components of developing an authentic and engaging preaching style:

- Finding your voice, reflecting your personality, beliefs, and values
- Being authentic and letting your true self shine in your sermons
- Paying attention to your delivery and presentation

Finding your voice can take time and practice but is essential for connecting with your audience and effectively conveying your message. Your preaching style should be engaging and dynamic, using storytelling, humor, and personal anecdotes to bring your message to life.

Establishing a connection with your audience is crucial in delivering a successful presentation. Here are some techniques to engage your audience:

- Maintaining eye contact, using open body language, and speaking with enthusiasm
- Using storytelling, humor, visual aids, and interactive elements to vary your delivery
- Catering to different learning styles by incorporating a variety of delivery techniques

NOTES

NOTES

Addressing Gender Discrimination in the Church

In this lesson, we will explore the issue of gender discrimination in the church and how it has affected women throughout history. We will examine the root causes of this discrimination, as well as the harmful effects it can have on individuals and the community as a whole. By understanding the dynamics of gender discrimination in the church, we can work towards creating a more inclusive and equitable religious environment for all.

We will also discuss strategies for addressing gender discrimination in the church, including promoting gender equality in leadership roles, challenging harmful stereotypes and biases, and supporting women's voices and contributions within the religious community. By taking proactive steps to address gender discrimination, we can help create a more welcoming and empowering church environment for everyone, regardless of gender.

Through this lesson, we hope to raise awareness about the importance of gender equality in the church and inspire individuals to take action to combat discrimination within their religious community. By working together to address these issues, we can create a more inclusive and equitable church environment that honors the dignity and worth of all individuals.

Key Lesson Concepts:

- Explore the root causes of gender discrimination in the church
- Discuss the harmful effects of discrimination on individuals and the community
- Strategies for promoting gender equality and challenging stereotypes in the church
- Encouraging support for women's voices and contributions within the religious community
- Raising awareness and taking action to create a more inclusive and equitable church environment

Building Confidence as a Female Preacher

Being a female preacher can come with its own set of challenges, but it is important to remember that your gender should not hinder your ability to deliver powerful and impactful sermons. In this lesson, we will explore strategies and techniques to help you build confidence in your preaching abilities and overcome any self-doubt that may arise.

One key aspect of building confidence as a female preacher is to focus on honing your skills and expertise. Take the time to study the Bible deeply, cultivate your speaking abilities, and practice your sermons regularly. Confidence often comes from feeling prepared and knowledgeable, so investing in your personal and spiritual growth can significantly boost your confidence as a preacher.

Additionally, it is important to surround yourself with a supportive community of fellow preachers and mentors who can provide encouragement and feedback. Having a strong support system can help you navigate any challenges that may arise and can boost your confidence as you continue to develop your preaching style. Remember, your voice as a female preacher is valuable and deserving of recognition – embrace your uniqueness and let your confidence shine through in your sermons.

Key Lesson Concepts:
- Focus on honing your skills and expertise
- Practice regularly and study the Bible deeply
- Build a supportive community of mentors and fellow preachers
- Embrace your uniqueness as a female preacher

Section Summary

In this lesson, we delve into the issue of gender discrimination within the church, its historical impact on women, root causes, and effects on individuals and the community:
- Explore the root causes of gender discrimination in the church.

- Discuss the harmful effects of discrimination on individuals and the community.
- Strategies for promoting gender equality and challenging stereotypes in the church.
- Encouraging support for women's voices and contributions within the religious community.
- Raising awareness and taking action to create a more inclusive and equitable church environment.

For female preachers, confidence and overcoming challenges are key. Strategies to help build confidence and deliver powerful sermons include:

- Focus on honing skills and expertise, study the Bible deeply.
- Practice preaching regularly to boost confidence.
- Build a supportive community of mentors and fellow preachers for encouragement and feedback.
- Embrace your uniqueness as a female preacher and let your confidence shine through.

NOTES

NOTES

Finding Mentorship and Support

In this lesson, we will explore the importance of finding mentorship and support in both professional and personal endeavors. Having a mentor can provide valuable guidance, insight, and encouragement, while having a support system can help you navigate challenges and celebrate achievements. By understanding where to look for mentorship and how to cultivate a support network, you can enhance your growth and success.

One key aspect of finding mentorship and support is identifying individuals who possess the knowledge, experience, and qualities you admire and aspire to emulate. This may include seeking out mentors within your industry or community who can offer valuable advice and perspective. Additionally, building a support network of friends, colleagues, or peers who can provide encouragement and assistance during both highs and lows can be incredibly beneficial.

Remember that mentorship and support are reciprocal relationships - just as you seek guidance and help from others, be open to providing mentorship and support to those who may benefit from your experience and expertise. By fostering these connections and relationships, you can create a strong community of individuals who are committed to helping each other succeed.

Key Lesson Concepts:
- Identify individuals who possess the knowledge and qualities you admire
- Build a support network of friends, colleagues, or peers
- Be open to providing mentorship and support in return

Utilizing Technology in Preaching

Technology has become an essential tool for communication in today's digital age, and the same applies to preaching. Utilizing technology in preaching can help reach a wider audience, engage church members in innovative ways, and enhance the overall worship experience. From livestreaming sermons to creating dynamic visual presentations, there are countless ways technology can be incorporated into preaching.

One key aspect of utilizing technology in preaching is the ability to adapt to different platforms and formats. Whether it's through social media, podcasts, or online streaming services, it's important for preachers to be versatile in how they deliver their messages. Additionally, technology can aid in research and preparation, allowing preachers to access a wealth of resources and tools to enhance their sermons.

Overall, embracing technology in preaching can help churches stay relevant in an increasingly digital world. By leveraging the power of technology, preachers can connect with their congregation on a deeper level, foster community engagement, and ultimately spread their message to a larger audience.

Key Lesson Concepts:

- Reach a wider audience
- Engage church members in innovative ways
- Enhance the worship experience
- Adapt to different platforms and formats
- Utilize technology for research and preparation
- Stay relevant in a digital world

Section Summary

In this lesson, we will delve into the significance of seeking mentorship and support for professional and personal growth:

- Having a mentor offers valuable guidance, insight, and encouragement.
- A supportive network helps navigate challenges and celebrate achievements.
- Finding mentorship and support enhances growth and success.
- Identify individuals with knowledge, experience, and qualities you admire.

- Build a support network with friends, colleagues, or peers for encouragement.
- Reciprocate mentorship and support to create a strong community.

Technology is an essential tool for communication and preaching in today's digital age, providing various benefits:

- Technology helps reach a broader audience and engage church members innovatively.
- Enhances the worship experience by incorporating dynamic visual presentations.
- Preachers need to adapt to different platforms like social media and podcasts.
- Utilize technology for research and preparation to enhance sermon quality.
- Embracing technology in preaching aids in staying relevant in the digital world.

NOTES

NOTES

Reflecting on Your Journey as a Female Preacher

As a female preacher, it is important to take the time to reflect on your journey and the experiences that have shaped you. This process of reflection allows you to gain insight into your strengths, weaknesses, and areas for growth. By reflecting on your journey, you can better understand your calling and purpose as a preacher, and identify ways to continue developing and honing your skills.

During this lesson, we will explore the significance of self-reflection in the context of being a female preacher. We will discuss the importance of introspection, self-awareness, and self-care in your journey. Through guided reflection exercises and discussions, you will have the opportunity to gain a deeper understanding of yourself, your preaching style, and your role in your community.

By the end of this lesson, you will have a clearer sense of who you are as a female preacher, and how your experiences have shaped you. You will also have practical strategies for continuing to reflect on your journey, and ways to leverage this reflection for personal and spiritual growth. Remember, reflecting on your journey is an ongoing process that can help you evolve and thrive as a preacher.

Key Lesson Concepts:
- Importance of self-reflection in the context of being a female preacher
- Significance of introspection, self-awareness, and self-care in your journey
- Practical strategies for continuing to reflect on your journey for personal and spiritual growth

Empowering Others in Homiletics

In this course, we will focus on empowering individuals to confidently deliver impactful homilies that inspire and engage their audience. Homiletics is the art of preaching or writing sermons, and by empowering others in this field, we are not only enhancing their public speaking skills but also enabling them to share meaningful messages that resonate with listeners.

Throughout this lesson, we will explore various techniques and strategies for empowering others in homiletics. From crafting compelling narratives to delivering with passion and conviction, we will cover the essential elements that contribute to effective preaching. By fostering a supportive and encouraging environment, we aim to help individuals develop their unique voice and style as homilists.

Key Lesson Concepts:

- Understanding the importance of empowering others in homiletics
- Exploring techniques for crafting compelling narratives in sermons
- Encouraging individuals to develop their unique voice and style as homilists

Section Summary

As a female preacher, reflecting on your journey is crucial for personal and spiritual growth. Here are key points to consider:

- Self-reflection helps in understanding strengths, weaknesses, and areas for growth.
- It aids in comprehending your calling, purpose, preaching style, and role in the community.
- Importance of introspection, self-awareness, and self-care.
- Guided reflection exercises to gain deeper self-understanding.
- Practical strategies for personal and spiritual growth.

Empowering individuals in homiletics is essential for impactful preaching. Here are important aspects to focus on:

- Homiletics is the art of preaching or writing sermons.
- Enhancing public speaking skills to share meaningful messages.
- Techniques for crafting compelling narratives and delivering with passion.

- A supportive environment for developing a unique voice and style as homilists.

NOTES

NOTES

Made in the USA
Middletown, DE
17 August 2024

59312961R00027